796.6   Porter, A   P
Por
          Greg LeMond, premier
          cyclist

GREG LEMOND

THE ACHIEVERS

GREG LEMOND

PREMIER CYCLIST

A. P. Porter

 Lerner Publications Company ■ Minneapolis

ACKNOWLEDGMENTS

Photographs are reproduced through the courtesy of: Keifel Sportfolio, pp. 1, 6, 8, 32, 56, 59; VeloNews/H. A. Roth, pp. 2, 3; Earl Wooster High School, p. 12; Bettmann Archive, pp. 14, 15, 16; John Howard, p. 19; Rodale Press, Inc., Photography Department, T. L. Gettings, pp. 20, 24; United States Cycling Federation, p. 23; The Southland Corporation, p. 27; Presse Sports/L'Équipe, pp. 31, 49; VeloNews/John Pierce, pp. 35, 51; VeloNews/Cor Vos, pp. 39, 40, 41, 42, 45, 46, 47; Star Tribune, Minneapolis-Saint Paul, pp. 54, 61; Richard Trombley, p. 64. Front and back covers: Keifel Sportfolio.

LIBRARY OF CONGRESS CATALOGING-IN-PUBLICATION DATA

Porter, A.P.
    Greg LeMond, premier cyclist / A.P. Porter.
    p.   cm.   —(The Achievers)
    Summary: Describes the training, competitions, and triumphs of the first American to win the Tour de France bicycle race.
    ISBN 0-8225-0476-6 (lib. bdg.)
    1. LeMond, Greg, 1961-   —Juvenile literature. 2. Cyclists —United States—Biography—Juvenile literature. 3. Tour de France (Bicycle race)—Juvenile literature. [1. LeMond, Greg, 1961-   . 2. Bicyclists.] I. Title. II. Series.
GV1051.L45P67   1989
796.6'092—dc20
[B]
[92]   89-13700
                                                         CIP
                                                          AC

Manufactured in the United States of America

International Standard Book Number: 0-8225-0476-6
Library of Congress Catalog Card Number: 89-13700

1 2 3 4 5 6 7 8 9 10 99 98 97 96 95 94 93 92 91 90

Contents

1 The Speed of LeMond 7

2 Getting in Gear 11

3 Fast Company 29

4 Cranking It Up 43

5 Shot Down 53

6 Back on the Saddle 57

Diagram of a Race 62

A Pronunciation Guide 63

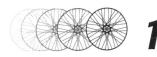

The Speed of LeMond

The *Tour de France* is the ultimate bicycle race. Every summer this grueling, three-week contest takes the world's greatest cyclists through 2,000 miles (3,218 kilometers) of French countryside. After all the stages (segments), victory goes to the rider with the best cumulative time.

On July 23 Greg LeMond was in second place, and his chances for victory in the 1989 Tour de France were slim. With only one stage left, LeMond was 50 seconds behind the leader, Frenchman Laurent Fignon. To win, Greg would have to make up his 50-second deficit in one 15.2-mile (24.5-km) time trial—a race against the clock. No racer had ever gained so much time in so little distance. The experts thought Fignon's lead was insurmountable. So much for the experts.

Greg and his elder son, Geoffrey

Greg was no stranger to overwhelming challenges. In 1983 he had taken the professional cycling world by storm by becoming the first American to win the World Professional Championship road race. In 1986 he had become the first American to win the Tour—a race ruled by Europeans since it began in 1903. In 1987 Greg had faced even tougher odds when a hunting accident nearly killed him. Greg had pulled through, although doctors had thought he might never race again. Once more Greg had defied the odds: Just two years after his near-fatal accident, he was within reach of his second Tour de France victory.

Everything rested on stage 21, the time trial into Paris. As he rolled down the starting ramp, Greg was as ready as he could get. He was geared for speed. Greg used a special handlebar to improve his aerodynamic position—so he would slip through the air more smoothly. Rather than spokes, his rear wheel was made from a disk, which would also decrease wind resistance. His riding suit fit snugly. He wore a teardrop-shaped helmet that would slice through the air and enable him to save a much as one second per kilometer.

Covering over 10 yards (9.1 meters) with each turn of the pedals, Greg averaged 34 miles per hour (54.7 km/h) for over 15 miles (24.1 km). It was the fastest any man had ever ridden in a Tour time trial. But Fignon was racing next. Even if he finished 49 seconds slower than Greg, he would still win the Tour.

Millions watched breathlessly as Fignon took off on his final ride, confident that he would hang on to his victory. It soon became clear that he couldn't.

Desperately, Fignon raced down the *Champs Élysées*. Agony swept across his face when he realized that his 50-second margin would not be enough. Fignon collapsed and fell from his bicycle at the finish line. LeMond had won the stage by 58 seconds. In a race that is normally won by minutes—even hours—Greg LeMond had won by a mere 8 seconds, the smallest margin of victory ever.

"I just went all out," Greg explained after the race. "I thought I could win, but I knew I needed something special. I didn't think. I just rode."

Greg rode, all right, the way he's been riding since he discovered bicycle racing in 1975.

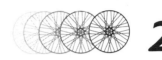 **2**

Getting in Gear

Bob LeMond, Greg's father, moved the family from near Long Beach, California, to Lake Tahoe in 1968, when Greg was seven years old. In Tahoe Greg explored the mountains, first gliding down them on a layer of snow as a freestyle skier and then climbing them on a bicycle, struggling to keep up with his athletic father.

Born June 26, 1961, Greg started skiing at seven and a half. By the time he was nine, he and his dad had discovered the best slopes in the Sierra Nevadas. The LeMonds—Bob, Bertha, Kathy, Greg, and Karen (a champion gymnast)—then moved across the border to Washoe Valley, Nevada, where Bob thought his real estate business would be more successful. In this, as in many other matters, Bob LeMond was right.

Greg was also a hunter, fly fisherman, and back-packer. But mostly, he was a skier—a good one, even before 1975, when he went to Wayne Wong's freestyle skiing camp in Vancouver, Canada. Wong was the number-one freestyle skier in the world. Wayne told Greg that he could improve his hotdogging (acrobatic skiing) by cycling in the off-season.

Greg decided that if cycling would help his skiing, he'd put up with it. In 1975 Greg LeMond thought of cycling as drudgery. He was 14 years old at the time, though, and impressionable. By September Greg and his father were cycling 20 miles (32.2 km) a day.

Greg's spot in the Wooster High yearbook listed no activities— racing took all of his extra time.

That summer of 1975, Bob and Greg climbed into the family van and chased a bicycle race into the mountains. John Howard and George Mount were riding for the United States Cycling Team against some of the best riders in the country. Mount and Howard were the hottest U.S. riders on the road in those days, and Greg saw close up what effort it took to ride a bicycle uphill.

Riding aggressively from the start, Mount and Howard dropped the pack on the first climb, leaving the rest of the riders with 60 hilly miles (96.5 hilly km) to go. Greg was impressed. "The fitness required is what really attracted me to cycling," he says.

Greg did what any 14-year-old with a new interest might do. He read about racing—the Tour de France, the toughest and longest stage race; the *Giro d'Italia*, the Tour of Italy, one of the most scenic races; the *Vuelta d'España*, the Spanish national tour. He read about the one-day classics—*Paris-Roubaix, Blois-Chaville, Grand Prix des Nations*.

He read about racers—Coppi, Anquetil, Taylor, Goullet, Bobet, and Eddy Merckx—king of the hill.

He read about nutrition and cleared the family kitchen of white flour and sugar. He read magazines and hung around bicycle shops.

Greg entered his first club race with the Reno (Nevada) Wheelmen in 1976. In that contest, his second-rate equipment hampered his performance, and his second-place finish made his natural ability obvious. Greg's dad said, "He just instantly knew what to do. He knows what it takes to win. All of his aggressions come out when he's on his bike."

"The first ride he went on he was like a pro of ten years," said Roland Della Santa, a racer and mechanic. "He was not only strong, he was smart. He had a real tactical mind—road racing is like playing chess at thirty miles per hour."

Like Greg, Jacques Anquetil was a master of smooth pedaling. Here Anquetil wins a classic race in 1957.

Greg dreamed of winning the Tour de France, as one of his heroes, Fausto Coppi, has just done here in 1949.

"You've got a lot of talent, guy," Della Santa told Greg, "but you should get a real racing bike." Greg and his father thought that was sound advice and went to a local bike shop to load up. Bob and Greg had found a sport that was an even better fit for them than skiing.

The bicycle salesman said, "No way, no. Never get a racing bike, kid. It's just too hard, you'll never stay in it." Nothing more has been heard from that salesman since.

Greg's new racing bike shone yellow and jewellike, more finely made than any bicycle Greg had ever ridden. His black wool shorts with a chamois leather lining fit like a fuzzy second skin. His cleated shoes gleamed.

Greg was a real bicycle racer, with real racing equipment. To prove it, he entered a real race, a 10-mile (16.1-km) criterium (a lap race) in Sacramento. He raced as an Intermediate against other boys 13 to 15 years old and beat all of them.

In fact, Greg thought winning was too easy, so he got permission to ride with the Juniors (16- to 19-year-olds). Junior races were longer than Intermediate races, and the packs were bigger.

Junior racers, bigger and stronger than he, loomed over Greg. Because of his age, Greg was limited to the smaller Intermediate gears. He had to pedal faster than the more experienced Juniors, who, with bigger gears, could pedal more slowly and travel at the same speed. The competition was much tougher than ever before. Greg loved it.

Greg admired Eddy Merckx's climbing ability. Merckx is the only man to win the Tour de France three years in a row.

Rather than being discouraged by the Intermediate gearing restrictions, Greg learned to pedal faster, which gave him a rounder and smoother stroke. He began to develop the power and suppleness demanded by high-level racing.

Every weekend the family would go off to a bike race, fueled by one of Bertha's special high-carbohydrate meals for sustained energy. Greg and his dad often entered the same races in different categories.

When the 1976 Nevada City Classic began, the temperature was over 100°F (38°C). Ten thousand spectators watched as the bunch unraveled from the back, with riders tiring and being dropped by the pack in the heat.

No Intermediate rider had ever won the Nevada City Junior race. No Intermediate won it in 1976, either. Clark Natwick, a third-year Junior, won the category. Little Greg LeMond, a 14-year-old rookie Intermediate, was second.

Greg realized then that he could ride with the best, maybe even straight up an Alpine pass, like Eddy Merckx, who had won five Tours de France. Because of the way he would overtake other riders and leave them in his wake, fans called Merckx "the Cannibal." Could Greg be a cannibal too?

Roland Della Santa thought so. Della Santa built Greg's first custom bike and encouraged Greg's dream— to be the best professional bicycle racer in the world.

When Greg started racing, John Howard (right) was one of the best in the U.S.

When Greg LeMond, local fast guy, hung around his shop, Della Santa told him stories of the great European cycling stars and the races they rode.

Della Santa talked about the Tours and Giri in the early twentieth century—when riders had no mechanics or spare parts and did their own repairs— even welding; when a rider simply rode as long as possible and slept along the way; when sabotage was common and more than one gear on a bicycle was illegal.

Greg stepped up his training. He grew bigger and stronger. He rode for hours each day, toughening his muscles, increasing his endurance, putting in his miles, and paying his dues. Tutoring and correspondence courses let him keep up with his classwork back at Wooster High.

Racing fans began to hear about this Nevada rocket. The Sierra Nevada Sportswriters and Broadcasters Association (SNSBA) named Gregory James LeMond "Prep of the Year." It was January 1977.

In April an administrative error listed Greg with the Seniors (ages 19 to 34) in California's Tour of San Joaquin. Riding with the Seniors meant riding with the fastest racers in the event, including John Howard, leader of the Exxon team, and Bob LeMond, who had become a champion racer on his own. Greg had seen Howard ride uphill and knew why he was the top road cyclist in North America. Howard had raced in three Olympics. He had won the Pan American Games road race, five national titles, and the first two Red Zinger Colorado Classics (later renamed the Coors Classic).

Pedaling faster than his opponents because of the gearing difference, Greg beat everybody but John Howard. The race comprised a 50-mile (80.5-km) road race, a 10-mile (16.1-km) time trial, and another 68-mile (109.4-km) road race. At the end, Greg lost to Howard by only six seconds. He was 15 years old.

The SNSBA named him Athlete of the Month of April 1977. Fans called him the "Phenom from Nevada."

John Howard said years later, "He was just fifteen and he was already destroying the top northern California Senior 1 riders. It was a two-day race in Fresno, a tough, hilly road race. He was with me the whole time. The two of us broke away, but instead of getting weaker the way most Juniors do, he got stronger and he was actually carrying me.

"I zapped him in the sprint and he probably learned from that. I predicted then that he would win a world championship. I had never seen a Junior like him."

Roland Della Santa's stories had sunk in, and Greg knew that the best riders and toughest races were in Europe. One night, Greg listed his cycling goals:

He planned to be the Junior national champion in 1977. He wanted to do well in the Junior World Championship in 1978. He planned to *win* the Junior World Championship in 1979 and the Olympic road race in 1980. He would turn professional in 1981. Greg was a dreamer.

In July 1977, Bob and Greg were both SNSBA Athletes of the Month. Greg won the Junior National Road Racing Championship and was the top qualifier for the U.S. Junior World Championship team. Greg's dad, meanwhile, set a U.S. amateur record for 25 miles (40.2 km). The LeMonds were quite a duo.

Eddie Borysewicz—"Eddie B."

In 1977 Greg was spotted by Eddie Borysewicz, the new coach of the U.S. Cycling Federation. "A diamond," Borysewicz said.

Bob and Greg LeMond in 1978

"Eddie B." became Greg's first real coach. He overlooked Greg's pigeon-toed stroke and saw a talented, dedicated athlete who loved the sport enough to work at it. Borysewicz put Greg on a training regimen and helped him enter Swiss and Belgian races in 1978. Greg even raced in a Junior stage race in Poland.

Greg continued to improve in 1978, winning the Junior National Championship and finishing only seconds behind the winner at the World Championship road race. At the Butterfly Criterium, he lapped the field, including the national sprint champion and a former Junior world champion. In May, Greg and the Senior road racing champion had a showdown at the Cat's Hill Criterium in California. Greg won.

24

Competitive Cycling Magazine said of LeMond, "Not just the best Junior prospect in years, but the best American prospect period."

On June 26, 1978, Greg spent his 17th birthday riding against the best Soviet and East German Junior riders in the Junior World Cycling Championship road race in Washington, D.C. After 76 miles (122.3 km) and almost three hours, the pack was still tightly bunched. To Greg's disadvantage, the course was only slightly hilly, not tough enough to break things loose. After forcing his way from the back of the 25-rider pack, Greg, riding for the Reno Wheelmen, managed ninth in the mass sprint to the finish line, the best any U.S. cyclist had ever done.

By September, Greg was dominating the Senior 1s and 2s—the best amateurs in the country. Greg LeMond won 29 races in 1978, including the Junior National Championship and 9 races in Europe. The competition was getting tougher all the time for Greg, and he was doing better than ever.

In 1979, after some early-season races in Europe, Greg returned home and became the first Junior rider to win the Tour of Nevada City.

All season Greg was aiming at the World Championships in Argentina. He had two years of hard European racing under his belt, and that experience made all the difference. Senior racing in the U.S. wasn't even as hard as the *Junior* racing in Belgium, and in 1979 Greg was the number-one Junior racer in Belgium.

In Argentina, Greg was entered in three races, including a new event for him—the 3,000-meter (1.9-mile) pursuit.

"It really was kind of a last-minute deal," Greg said. "The morning of the race I got on the track and set up my position and rode for half an hour to get used to it. Jim Grill, the U.S. track coach, showed me how to start. That evening was my first track race this year. . . . I went as fast as I could."

A velodrome's smooth surface and steep banking allow speeds over 40 miles (64.4 km) per hour.

The pursuit is ridden on a velodrome—a bicycle track. The two racers start on opposite sides of the course and try to catch each other. Track bikes have no brakes (sudden stops are deadly on a velodrome), one gear, and direct drive (which means no coasting— if you're rolling, you're pedaling). For Greg LeMond, a bike is a bike, though, and he soon got the hang of it. He set a U.S. record and won the silver medal for second place in an event he'd never before raced in.

Two days later, Greg and his teammates, Jeff Bradley, Greg Demgen, and Ron Kiefel, won a bronze medal in the 70-kilometer (43.4-mile) team time trial— the first TTT medal ever for the United States.

Near the end of Greg's main event, the 120-kilometer (74.4-mile) road race, Greg and Belgian Kenny De Marteleire were all alone heading for the finish on a large automobile-racing track. In desperation, De Marteleire pushed Greg onto the infield and smack into a barrier of old auto tires.

Greg's superb bike handling was all that saved him. He swerved frantically and managed to get back on the track. As Greg was about to overtake De Marteleire, the Belgian pushed Greg onto the infield again. Greg came back on the track a second time, but couldn't catch his opponent before the finish line. De Marteleire's actions hadn't escaped the officials' notice, though, and he was disqualified. Greg was declared the winner.

Greg LeMond became the first U.S. rider to win a gold medal in the Junior World Championship road race. He was a member of the first U.S. team to win a medal in the team time trial and the only person to win three medals in World Championship competition. Greg LeMond was 18.

The winter of 1979-80 was pivotal for Greg. He was the Junior world champion. He'd already raced in Europe, getting his feet wet gradually over the previous two years. He was looking forward to his last amateur races in the Olympics and to turning professional soon after. Then the U.S. government announced its boycott of the 1980 Summer Olympics, putting Greg's Olympic hopes out of reach. Greg wanted to become a professional right away, but Borysewicz tried to dissuade him. Cycling for money meant moving to Europe, and that was more than Eddie B. thought Greg was ready for.

Greg thought differently. He had paid his dues and had nothing left to prove in the U.S. He felt that the only way for him to do better was to take on the best in the world, and the best in the world were in Europe.

 **3**

Fast Company

Greg LeMond was the Junior world champion, but still little known outside the U.S. Many a world champion had come and gone without making a dent in the professional ranks. Greg needed to attract the attention of the managers and coaches of pro racing teams.

Unlike most European races, the *Circuit de la Sarthe* is open to both professionals and amateurs. The U.S. National Team entered this stage race in western France to train, not to win. Greg won anyway. He became the youngest rider and the first American to win a major European pro-am race.

Cyrille Guimard, a French cycling coach, had been following Greg's career for a year or so. Greg's victory in Sarthe persuaded Guimard to see this LeMond.

The last day of the 1980 *Ruban Granitier Breton* race was one of Greg's worst. He was four minutes ahead of the pack, riding with the Soviet team in a breakaway—a group that has pulled ahead of the rest of the field. Greg was in a good spot to win the race when he got a flat tire.

As he waited several minutes for his team car to bring him a fresh wheel, Greg saw his chances for victory disappear down the road like the Soviets. By the time his mechanic showed up, Greg was livid. The mechanic's fumbling with the replacement wheel was too much. Greg threw his bicycle at the team car and quit the race. Guimard saw the whole thing.

"You have the fire to be a great champion," Guimard told Greg. He liked Greg's spirit and later offered him a job for the 1981 season. Guimard had a reputation for developing young racers. He had brought Lucien Van Impe to a Tour de France victory and had turned Bernard Hinault into the world's best cyclist.

Back in Paris, after six hours of negotiation and several phone calls to his father for advice, Greg signed his first professional cycling contract in July of 1980. Greg chose the Renault-Elf-Gitane team for a base salary of about $40,000 a year—not bad for a 19-year-old's first job.

Greg had a hard first year in Europe. In the winter of 1980–81, he had married Kathy Morris, whom he had met at a bicycle race in Milwaukee, Wisconsin.

Riding for Renault, Greg won the 1982 Tour de l'Avenir.

A pack rolls along between fields of sunflowers.

Their time together in LaCrosse, Wisconsin, had been romantic and restful, and when Greg got to Europe, he was 15 pounds overweight.

Guimard had arranged housing for Greg and Kathy in Nantes, France. The newlyweds spent six weeks in a tiny hotel room, waiting for their house. When they moved in, they had no furniture, no hot water, and no heat. There was no kitchen. And they were homesick.

"I didn't speak any French. It was wet, rainy, and cloudy all the time," Greg said. The rain, wind, and overcast skies damped his enthusiasm, and his training suffered. His daily mileage dropped from 90 miles (144.8 km) to 60 miles (96.5 km). His physical condition got worse.

Greg's first professional race, the *Étoile de Bessèges,* was a nightmare. After a 300-mile (482.7-km) trip in the team bus, Greg was carsick, exhausted, and in lousy shape. In the race, he got dropped from the pack right away. The racers' speeds were unbelievable.

Guimard said, "Boy, you've got to train. You've got to lose some of that weight, you're just too heavy."

After the race, Greg rode another 30 miles (48.3 km) for good measure. In the next day's race, he got dropped twice. He rode 40 extra miles (64.4 extra km) that day.

Greg and Kathy slowly adjusted—to France, to the food, and to a foreign culture. It had taken 10 weeks just to get their house in order. Now Greg was riding better, and Kathy's rock-solid support was making a difference in Greg's attitude. Greg sometimes had doubts; Kathy never did.

Three months after Greg's professional start, he won the *Tour de l'Oise,* his first professional victory. He began to regain his confidence. He really could ride with the best.

In the *Dauphiné Libéré,* Greg raced against Bernard Hinault over some of the mountains he would one day face in the Tour de France. Hinault was at his peak, and Greg stayed with him to finish third overall. Greg could climb with the best.

In June, Greg used some of that climbing skill in the Coors Classic, the biggest stage race in the U.S.

The Coors Classic also took Greg and Kathy home again—to be with family instead of strangers, to speak English instead of halting French, and to eat familiar food instead of things they couldn't pronounce.

"[In the 1981 Coors Classic] I planned on breaking away early," Greg said. "I wanted to string out the field. This course doesn't allow team tactics. There is no drafting (riding closely behind another rider to reduce wind resistance). It becomes an individual race." On the fifth day, Greg took the lead and went on to win the overall men's title.

"Suicide's my kind of hill," Greg said of the monstrous "Suicide Hill," where he had pulled away from the competition. "That's where I won the race. I'd like to see even steeper hills in the next race." Steeper hills were on the way.

Meanwhile, Greg LeMond was becoming a celebrity. "In the U.S., I get embarrassed to tell people I'm a bike racer." But racing fans in Europe were beginning to recognize *l'Américain.*

"They send things for me to sign. 'Oh, you're the American,' they say. Bicycle racers in Europe are sort of like pro football players in America. In Europe, it's different. Bicycle racers are on television and in the newspapers every day. The public sees them a lot."

In the *Liège-Bastogne-Liège* race, "There was a lot of traffic, about three hundred riders. It was raining and only about thirty-two degrees.

Greg looked tanned and fit in the '84 Tour de France.

"I turned my head and the peloton (pack) stopped. My brakes didn't work because ice had built up," Greg explained. His handlebar hooked with another rider's, and both racers fell. Greg was out of action for two months with a broken collarbone.

There was no Coors Classic for Greg in 1982. No Nevada City race, either. There was the World Championship road race in Goodwood, England, though. A stomach virus had sapped Greg's energy, and he wasn't sure that he would even ride. Some of his family had come over from the United States, though, and, "Their airline tickets weren't redeemable, so I felt obliged to race," Greg said.

Five hundred yards (457.2 m) from the end, Jonathan Boyer, the only other American near the front, began to fade. Greg whipped past him, only to be nipped at the line by the Italian Giuseppe Saronni. Greg LeMond's silver medal for second place represented the best World Championship performance ever by a North American.

Greg's 1982 season peaked with the *Tour de l'Avenir,* a pro-am version of the Tour de France (which is for professional cyclists only). Greg dominated the entire race and won by a record 10 minutes. He was euphoric.

Greg's training rides—up to 100 miles (161 km) a day, five or six days a week—were paying off. He had been training and racing for some eight years, watching his diet, and listening to his *directeur sportif*—coach—now Cyrille Guimard. Now Greg was near the top and closing in on the big one—the Tour de France.

There was to be no Tour for Greg in 1983, though. He was riding better than ever, but the Tour is in a class by itself. Three weeks of grueling racing in all weather, over mountains, and against the wind and the finest professional racers anywhere require toughness, savvy, and experience. Guimard didn't think Greg was ready yet.

Greg and Kathy LeMond left Nantes in the winter of 1982-83. They settled in Kortrijk, Belgium, some

10 miles (16.1 km) north of the French border. Greg could get lots of good training races—from the North Sea to the hills of Flanders—and Kathy could speak English there and hear more English from neighbors and on television. The local stores even sold books and magazines in English.

In the early summer of 1983, Greg rode the Vuelta d'España. He had gotten off to a slow start that spring and hoped that Spain's weather would be good. He could then perhaps get into top shape fast. No such luck. It rained in Spain, and when it wasn't raining, it was cold. Bernard Hinault, the strongest Renault rider, had an injured knee, and the team was suffering without a leader.

Guimard told Greg to quit the race and go home to rest. Greg should then train in the Alps for the Dauphiné Libéré stage race, Guimard said.

Greg took Guimard's advice and trained around his home in Kortrijk, but nothing seemed to help his spirits or his condition. His morale was so low that he even considered quitting racing! When he decided that he was doing all he could, he relaxed. Instead of giving up racing, he gave up worrying—a much better idea.

In the Dauphiné Libéré, Pascal Simon of France won the eight-stage race by two minutes. Greg came in second. Simon was subsequently disqualified for using a chemical called Micorene. Greg then became the first American to win a major stage race.

The World Championship in Berne, Switzerland, capped the 1983 season for Greg. He thought he had a good shot at the title. He was right.

In the World Championship road race, Greg stayed near the front of the pack for 15 laps. On the 16th 9.4-mile (15.1-km) lap, Greg attacked and broke away. Italian Moreno Argentin and Spaniard Faustino Ruperez tried to stay with him, but couldn't. Greg accelerated, dropped both riders, and rode his last and fastest lap alone. Thinking that Argentin was still in the breakaway, the Italian team rode slowly at the front of the pack in order to block the other riders and enlarge Argentin's time gap. The Italians unintentionally increased Greg's margin of victory.

Greg LeMond became the first American to win the World Professional Championship. Greg had placed well in a lot of races in 1983, and he found himself in contention for the Super Prestige Pernod Trophy, which is given to the racer who has the most points for the entire season. If his streak continued, Greg could win two world titles in the same year.

Greg continued to do well—finishing fourth in the French classic (one-day race) Blois–Chaville, second in the Tour of Lombardy (he lost by a quarter of an inch), and second in the Grand Prix des Nations time trial. He clinched the Super Prestige Pernod Trophy and left for the U.S. exhausted and triumphant.

Greg had a good time that winter of 1983–84 and a much-needed rest. The rest ended in February 1984, when Kathy gave birth to their son, Geoffrey James LeMond. Fatherhood elated Greg, but the demands of caring for his newborn son hampered his training.

Greg, center, winning his first World Professional Championship for the United States in 1983

From left, Adri Van Der Poel (2nd place), Greg, and Stephen Roche (3rd place) after the '83 World Championship road race

The Tour de France—three weeks and 2,000 miles (3,218 km) of racing—was on his schedule for 1984, and Greg would need all the training he could get. The cold of the early season bothered Greg, and he was still overweight from the winter. The pressure of being the world champion and a favorite for the Tour de France was weighing heavily on Greg. He was nervous.

After the first few days of the Tour, Greg developed bronchitis. That, coupled with a severely inflamed foot, dimmed his Tour prospects. At the beginning of the last week, though, Greg was in eighth place and feeling better. During those final days, he even improved his standing by five places, finishing third overall. He won the *maillot blanc*—the white jersey awarded to the best rookie—an impressive showing.

Greg and his friend Phil Anderson (left) chat with a photographer during a break in the '84 Tour de France.

Sean Kelly, Phil Anderson, and Greg pick up the pace in the '84 Tour.

Third place in the world's most prestigious bicycle race is no big deal, though, when you've dreamed of the winner's yellow jersey—*maillot jaune*—for almost 10 years. He said, "I'd half-expected to win the thing."

Greg went home to the U.S. that winter still frustrated, and he vowed to prepare better for the 1985 Tour, perhaps with the Giro d'Italia. He'd learned a lot in his first Tour and now he knew that a three-week race was incredibly hard—physically, mentally, and emotionally.

42

4

Cranking It Up

In the 1984 Tour, Greg had been a *domestique,* a support rider who is expected to help the team leader, but not necessarily to win anything. Laurent Fignon was the Renault team's leader, having won the Tour in 1983 and 1984. Greg wanted to lead, not support someone else. When Bernard Hinault, four-time winner of the Tour and the number-one pro in the world, asked that he join him on the new *La Vie Claire* team, Greg hesitated.

Hinault assured Greg that they would share the team's leadership. Hinault also said that he would retire in November 1986, on his 32nd birthday—in effect making Greg his successor as team leader.

Bernard Tapie, owner of La Vie Claire, offered Greg a million dollars over three years. That would make Greg LeMond the highest-paid cyclist in the world. Greg said yes to La Vie Claire (which means "the good life"), but reluctantly. He'd have to leave his coach, Cyrille Guimard. Guimard had encouraged, coached, and developed Greg as a racer. Greg would miss him.

With La Vie Claire, Greg managed to complete the Paris-Roubaix race in the spring of 1985 with a fourth-place finish. He got third place in the Giro, while helping Hinault win. He and Hinault agreed that in the Tour the team would work for the stronger of the two of them—the one with the best chance to win. Hinault said, "Greg or me, it's all the same."

The 1985 Tour de France began on June 28. Twenty million people lined the roads, and 600 million watched on television. There would be 23 stages, 9 of them in the mountains.

Hinault took the lead right away. There were several early stages *contre la montre*—time trials against the clock. Hinault excelled at time trials.

Greg also rode well—by the 13th stage, he was in second place, 5 minutes, 23 seconds behind Hinault.

Then, 300 yards (274.3 m) from the finish of the St. Étienne stage, Hinault bumped Australian Phil Anderson and crashed headfirst to the ground. He bounced.

A muddy Greg after the '85 Paris–Roubaix classic

Greg pours it on in the Swiss Alps, followed by an official car.

With blood streaming down his face, Hinault remounted and rode slowly across the finish line, his nose fractured in two places. Asked if he could continue, Hinault said, "For the team, for my two kids, and for my wife, I've got to go on to win."

Over the next few days, Hinault grew weaker, and his lead over Greg shrank to under four minutes. He had a puffy face, black eyes, and bronchitis. He breathed with difficulty.

On July 16, Greg and the rest of the breakaway group led Hinault by over a minute for the stage as they topped a mountain pass. Greg had been riding hard, and Paul Koechli, La Vie Claire's coach, told Greg to back off and not leave Hinault so far behind. Hinault was still first overall, and Koechli didn't want him to lose any more time than necessary. Greg slowed down.

Greg, angry and tearful, argued with Koechli after the race. Greg said later, "If Hinault was in my place he would not have waited, that's all I have to say. . . . If I'd raced my own race I might have . . . won the Tour de France. I had to make a big sacrifice."

Greg confers with team staff during the '85 Tour.

The next night, Greg said, "The race is over with, really. I helped Hinault accomplish his goals this year, and he will help me accomplish mine next year."

Greg finished the 1985 Tour 1 minute, 42 seconds behind Hinault. Bob LeMond said, "It's a French team and a French race, and they wanted a French winner."

The press asked Bernard Hinault if he would try for a record sixth Tour win in 1986. He said, "Normally, this would be my last victory. There is a new generation coming, and it is time for the team to go on. But I will race one more year, and if I am in the Tour de France, I shall only compete to help one of my teammates win. It should be Greg LeMond. Next year, I will *make* Greg LeMond win."

When the 1986 Tour de France came around, Greg hadn't won a major European race since the 1983 World Championship. Laurent Fignon, Greg's former teammate and the Tour winner in 1983 and 1984, said, "Greg LeMond has all the physical qualities needed to win the Tour. But he doesn't have the mind-set of a winner." Famous last words.

Eleven days into the 1986 Tour, Greg was eighth overall; Hinault was third. Greg said, "He's not the Bernard Hinault of five years ago. I know in the last week of the race I'm going to be stronger than he is."

On the Tour's toughest day, a 116-mile grind over four mountains, Hinault broke away on the first descent and established a big lead. When Hinault went into the biggest of his 14 gears, Greg told himself, "He's trying to bury me." Hinault seemed to have forgotten his promise to work for Greg this year.

But Hinault bonked—his muscles ran out of fuel, and his body faced exhaustion. He began drifting aimlessly across the road.

Alexi Grewal of the 7-Eleven team said, "He was dead in the water, standing still. I thought, 'God, he's finished.' He didn't try to pedal. He didn't even see us go by."

Greg was in the group that overtook Hinault. Greg asked Hinault if he wanted him to stay behind and help. "I'm dead," Hinault croaked. "Follow the others."

Bernard Hinault and Greg wave to fans during the '86 Tour.

As the riders began their last climb of the stage—a 3,500-foot (1,066.8-m) ascent—rookie La Vie Claire rider Andy Hampsten attacked and pulled away. Greg bridged the gap and rode near Andy's rear wheel for shelter from the wind.

Earlier that year, in the Tour of Switzerland, Greg had stifled his own effort so Hampsten could win. Now Greg needed time to rest, and Andy was giving it to him.

Hampsten hurt all over. He hadn't eaten all day, and when a trainer gave him some food, he vomited. But he did the job he had been hired to do—help Greg LeMond win the Tour de France.

Greg got two and a half miles of shelter from the wind before Hampsten burned out. That was enough. Greg went on to win his first stage victory in the Tour de France, finishing four and a half minutes ahead of Hinault. On the next Alpine stage, Greg gained over three minutes more on Hinault and won the leader's yellow jersey.

Greg and Hinault rode together the next day, finishing the stage side by side with their hands clasped overhead. At the end, Greg allowed Hinault to win the stage by a wheel.

"I can only hope that the strongest man wins," Hinault said. Would he attack Greg, after promising to help him win, reporters asked? "Maybe so," Hinault said.

Greg responded, "Everybody on the team should be my ally now. This is the hardest Tour de France in 40 years, and not only do I have to defeat the pack, I have to race against my own team."

Greg needn't have worried. It was too late for Hinault to catch up, and three days before the end, Hinault conceded. Why had Hinault attacked in the mountains when he needn't have taken such a big chance? He said, "Cycling is a magnificent sport, but remember, it is also a game."

Hinault explained that he'd been giving Greg a racing lesson. "I've put Greg under the maximum pressure. If he didn't buckle, that means he's a champion and deserves to win the race. . . . I did it for his own good. Next year, maybe he'll have to fight off another opponent who will make life miserable for him. He'll know how to resist, how to fight back now."

Greg knew all he needed to know. He was the first non-European to win the world's premier bicycle race —the Tour de France.

5

Shot Down

In 1986 things were going well for Greg LeMond—former world champion, winner of the Tour de France, and the highest-paid bicycle racer in the world. The winter of 1986–87 was uneventful. But the following spring put an end to Greg's contentment.

While hunting wild turkey in California in April, Greg's brother-in-law mistook him for a bird. He fired his shotgun and hit Greg in the back with about 60 pellets. Forty miles from the nearest city, Greg LeMond lay bleeding on the ground.

"I was making Geoffrey breakfast, and the phone rang. They said, 'It's UC Davis Medical Center, and your husband has been shot,'" Kathy said. Nine months pregnant, she rushed to the hospital, and after a three-hour wait she saw Greg.

Kathy helped Greg through the tough times.

"They were lifting him up . . . and out of every single hole, blood was dripping. I couldn't believe that was him." Two weeks later, Kathy gave birth to their second child, Scott.

Even after hours of surgery, more than 30 pellets remained in Greg's body, six in the lining of his heart. Recovery was slow.

"I wondered if I would ever cycle again, let alone ride in the Tour de France," Greg said later. But even this near-fatal accident couldn't keep Greg off his bike. Slowly, he began training again.

Three painful months after the shooting, just as Greg was beginning to train hard, he needed an emergency appendectomy. That ended his season for good. Again, Greg had to start over. After a slow recovery, he resumed his training, but there was more trouble ahead.

In 1988, just after beginning to race for the PDM team, he crashed and injured a muscle sheath in his left leg.

"I kept getting cortisone injections in my leg, hoping for a quick cure. I wasn't healing. I didn't know why. It was more frustrating than after my gunshot wound. I could barely walk, let alone train."

So Greg went home to Minnesota, his new off-season base. He had surgery on his leg and was training again four days later! He had been suffering from injuries for almost two years, and his body had taken a lot of punishment, but he wouldn't let up.

"I had doubts about making it back," he admitted. "Not doubts exactly, more frustration. I would train well, do everything I thought was right. . . . Every time I raced I was always at my maximum and I was always dropped. That was the most difficult part. I expected to be right with the best of them right away.

I had won the Tour de France, and here I was being dropped by some guy riding back roads in California. And then, one day, I dropped *him*." Greg's comeback had begun.

In Europe, everybody likes bicycle racing.

6

Back on the Saddle

Greg began 1989 slowly. He entered races only to train, to try to stay with the pack. Greg was riding for ADR, a weak Belgian team. Racing insiders wondered if he would ever really recover. Many people said that Greg was through, that he was finished in bicycle racing. Some said that his having interests other than cycling—hunting, Nordic skiing, and golf, for instance—was a sign of his lack of dedication. But Greg was as determined to come back as he had been to race bicycles to begin with.

"The last two years have been the most humiliating of my life," Greg said. "Riders and team managers thought I was through, and that made me more determined than ever to return."

He still wasn't winning, though. Then, during the

Giro, Otto Jácome, Greg's *soigneur*—personal trainer —told him that he looked a little pale and suggested that he get a blood test for anemia—iron deficiency. Jácome's intuition was right.

"I took an iron supplement that night," Greg said some time later. "The next day I felt the improvement. Before that, on the smallest hill, I was gone."

In the Giro's last time trial, Greg placed second, better than he had done all year. He was finally looking forward to the 1989 Tour. He began to think he could match the competition.

Not only did he match it, he came from behind to upset Fignon and the experts' predictions in the fastest time trial in the Tour's history.

Again, Greg LeMond had won the Tour de France. Again he was the man to beat in any bicycle race he entered. He could propel himself at 34 miles (54.7 km) per hour for miles on end. He could climb mountains.

· A few weeks later in the World Professional Championship road race, Greg faced Fignon, Dmitri Konychev, and Sean Kelly in a sprint to the finish of the exhausting 161.1-mile (259.2-km) race. Greg had one of the best heart-lung systems ever examined. He had efficient muscles that could contract rhythmically for hours. He had tremendous energy and *very* little body fat to carry around. But Greg LeMond was no sprinter.

Fignon, Greg, and Delgado relax after Greg's stunning finish in the '89 Tour de France.

He sprinted anyway. With less than 250 yards (228.6 m) to go, Greg took the lead and held off Kelly's surge to win the World Championship for the second time. Amazing! Greg became the fourth man in history to win the Tour de France and the World Championship in the same year.

After his Tour win, Greg said, "I have put out one hundred percent the last two years: a heck of a lot of training, a heck of a lot of suffering, a heck of a lot of pain to get to where I am now. . . . I knew I would have the last say."

After his 1989 Tour win, Greg became a celebrity, even at home in Minnesota. At least people there don't hang around outside his home, the way they did in Belgium after the '86 Tour. Both Greg and Kathy are essentially shy and avoid the limelight whenever they can. When you're the best, though, you're likely to be famous, and media attention is part of the deal.

People have begun to recognize him on the street. Warner Brothers plans to make a movie about Greg's career. There are constant demands on his and Kathy's time and frequent invasions of their privacy—an unfortunate result of Greg's success. In October 1989, Kathy and Greg LeMond became the parents of their third child, Simone—more joy and work. They would like very much to live like normal people, but they can't, not anymore.

Greg always has time for racing fans.

In late 1989, Greg signed a three-year contract with the French "Z" team for $5.5 million. He wants to race until 1995 or so, and then retire. Since being named Sports Illustrated's 1989 "Sportsman of the Year," Greg is more famous than ever. He might as well get used to it. Gregory LeMond is the best—the world's premier cyclist.

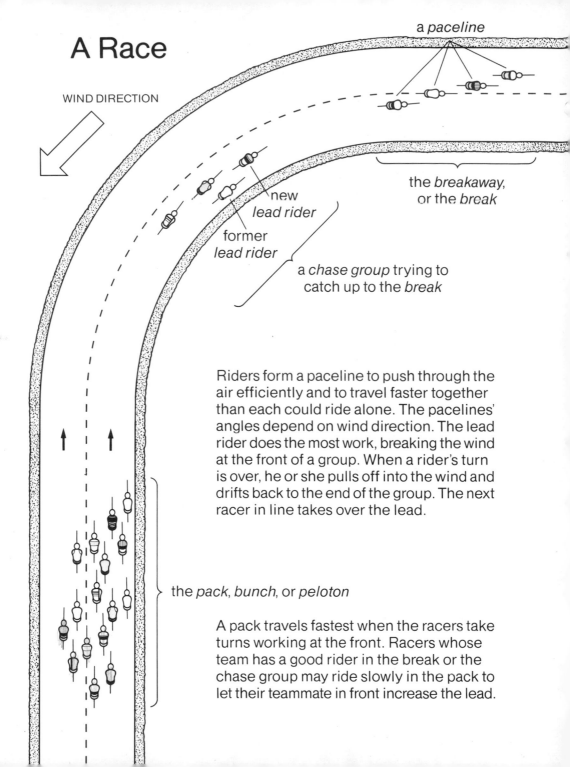

A Race

a *paceline*

WIND DIRECTION

the *breakaway*, or the *break*

new *lead rider*

former *lead rider*

a *chase group* trying to catch up to the *break*

Riders form a paceline to push through the air efficiently and to travel faster together than each could ride alone. The pacelines' angles depend on wind direction. The lead rider does the most work, breaking the wind at the front of a group. When a rider's turn is over, he or she pulls off into the wind and drifts back to the end of the group. The next racer in line takes over the lead.

the *pack*, *bunch*, or *peloton*

A pack travels fastest when the racers take turns working at the front. Racers whose team has a good rider in the break or the chase group may ride slowly in the pack to let their teammate in front increase the lead.

A Pronunciation Guide

Blois–Chaville	BLWAH shah-VEEL
Eddie Borysewicz	EH-dee BOH-ruhs-SEH-veech
Champs Élysées	SHAWN zay-lee-ZAY
Circuit de la Sarthe	seer-KWEE duh lah SAHRT
contre la montre	KOHN-truh lah MOHN-truh
Cyrille Guimard	see-REEL ghee-MAHR
Dauphiné Libéré	DOH-fee-NAY LEE-bay-RAY
directeur sportif	dee-rehk-TUHR spohr-TEEF
domestique	doh-meh-STEEK
Étoile de Bessèges	ay-TWAHL duh beh-SEHZH
Giro d'Italia	JEE-roh dee-TAHL-yah
Grand Prix des Nations	grahn PREE deh nah-SYOHN
Kortrijk	KOHRT-rike
l'Américain	lah-mehr-ee-CAN
Laurent Fignon	loh-RAWN fee-NYOHN
La Vie Claire	lah VEE KLEHR
Liège–Bastogne–Liège	lee-EHZH bahs-TOHN lee-EHZH
maillot blanc	my-YOH BLAWN
maillot jaune	my-YOH ZHOHN
Paris–Roubaix	pah-REE roo-BAY
Ruban Granitier Breton	roo-BAWN grah-nee-TYAY breh-TOHN
St. Étienne	san tay-TYEHN
soigneur	swah-NYUHR
Tour de France	TOOR duh FRAHNS
Tour de l'Avenir	TOOR duh lahv-NEER
Tour de l'Oise	TOOR duh LWAHZ
Vuelta d'España	VWEHL-tah deh-SPAH-nyah

ABOUT THE AUTHOR

A. P. Porter, in addition to being an experienced cyclist, has been a math tutor, banker, photography teacher, railroad brakeman, and bicycle mechanic. Born in Chicago, he now lives in Minneapolis, Minnesota, with two bikes and his favorite philodendron plant.